THE CROSS CORONA AND OTHER POEMS

BASA ENOCH ANAND ELEAZAR

Ukiyoto Publishing

All global publishing rights are held by

Ukiyoto Publishing

Published in 2024

Content Copyright ©BASA ENOCH ANAND ELEAZAR

ISBN 9789360494315

All rights reserved.

No part of this publication may be reproduced, transmitted, or stored in a retrieval system, in any form by any means, electronic, mechanical, photocopying, recording or otherwise, without the prior permission of the publisher.

The moral rights of the author have been asserted.

This is a work of fiction. Names, characters, businesses, places, events, locales, and incidents are either the products of the author's imagination or used in a fictitious manner. Any resemblance to actual persons, living or dead, or actual events is purely coincidental.

This book is sold subject to the condition that it shall not by way of trade or otherwise, be lent, resold, hired out or otherwise circulated, without the publisher's prior consent, in any form of binding or cover other than that in which it is published.

www.ukiyoto.com

Acknowledgments

At the very beginning, I express my deepest gratitude to our Father in heaven for the grace he has given me to publish this book.

I thank Rev. B. Samarpana Kiran for her prayers for me and my family. Four great elder brothers in the Lord who have been a blessing to me are Sri Makka Emmanuel, Rt. Rev. Dr.Nune Vinod Kumar, Sri Basa Krupanandam and Ganapuram Devadas.

To all the above four I express my gratitude from the depths of my heart for their prayers, guidance and support.

The pastorate committee of our church has always given its approval to the matters regarding financial and other help for me. So they too receive my profound thanks.

Just when I was scratching my head about who would do the typing work related to my poems, the kind Lord gave me Priyanka. Patient and obliging, she is a precious pearl and I am grateful to her for her tremendous effort. There are other relatives and friends, too numerous to mention here who have been a blessing to me. I am indebted to them for their love.

I thank the Ukiyoto publishers for their prompt responses to my queries and for giving me adequate time to double check my creative work. I express my deepest gratitude for their initiative, creativity, and energy in bringing out my poems in the form of a wonderful book.

Contents

The Enemy Within	1
Asking for the Special G	2
The Call of my Father	4
The Twin Blessings of the Creator	6
Sin and the Saviour	9
The Dimensions of the Cross	10
Silence is Gold	13
Have Lots, Will Speak	15
Dreams for a Daughter Dear	19
Breakfast Time Unshackled	21
Ground Zero	24
A Volatile Mix	26
Passing into Nothingness	28
Peace of God	30
The Way of Wisdom	32
The Rising Sun	34
Under His Wings	35
About the Author	*36*

The Enemy Within

The airlock in the main above blocks the flow of life-giving water
But O Lord let not the bubble of envy here inside
Mar the march of men to win and victory

Envy burned deep within Israel's king Saul
Who let go his whizzing spear
To impale Israel's future king

Let the Lord nip the cardinal sin in the bud
Pluck it out from within me
That I may not mar the march of men to triumph and glory

Is he the personification of pride and envy?
If so, let the saviour
Who on his knees washed the disciple's feet
Enter the red throbbing chamber of my filthy heart
To burst the bubble of death-dealing envy
So, unshackle me from hell's fire
That I may here and forever
Rejoice by my King's side
As indeed everywhere glory and victory are the Lord's alone!!

Asking for the Special G

Hurdles impossible for men to cross
Are mere twigs to bend and break
And burn to make a bonfire of the wooden pile
And offer once again to my Lord
My body and my entire being
And then to march ahead
With the cross of Christ held aloft!

Doesn't the one above
Look for a grateful heart
For the mighty deeds done
In the centuries past and in the challenging present?

How can we leave the maker's hand empty
And walk away as if no event occurred?
And as if no blessing was bestowed?

O God of the generous blessing
Let me never be
Like the nine lepers with empty hearts and songdead lips
Who went their unvoiced and witless way
And did not their steps reverse
To render to you a heartfelt and a sincere thanks

So O God who hears his children's prayers
A grateful heart your servant grant
And of your spirit pour on me a double measure
That I may bring forth
Fruit plentiful for your glory's sake!

The Call of my Father

The call of my father is heard no more
In my little home of love
Why does it not reverberate again
In my little home of love?

When he called me – his little pet of twelve
Countless time in sweet heart warming tones
My heart leapt with joy

Why did my cup of loss overflow so early in life
When I was just at the cusp of my teens?

Why did the iron hand of fate
Gag my father's voice forever?
Why did the cruel hand of fate
Snatch that gentle voice so early?
To swell the choir of praise in the hall of heaven?

Now I make rounds of the streets of silence
Seeking that one call
That touches me with the whiff of your love

Oh who can breach that thick impenetrable wall of silence
That cleaves only on the other side of eternity

BASA ENOCH ANAND ELEAZAR

How I wish that the call of my father
Punches a hole in the ceiling of the sky
That I may hear one more time
My father's voice from on high

So now I carry your memories dear father
Like the labourer carrying his pile of bricks on his head

When daddy is heard
From a child's lips in a hall
And when you do not make an appearance
I swallow the silence
And retrace my crestfallen frame
To my chair at the rear
And bow my head in silent prayer

The Twin Blessings of the Creator

Faith and reason are by the wise God given
Inseparable like Jonathan and David
They walk hand in hand
Ready to bless the sick and the sinner

Those who chop and throw reason away
Turn it into a nonagenarian hobbling on a broken stick
And folks who attack faith with a vengeance
And fling it into the air
End up with the smog of short sightness in their own eyes

Then why should anyone many a time
Disdain logic and at other times the Logos
As if dishing out justice?

And then to deny the fabulous op
Of nursing the sick and saving the souls

Why can't there be the blessed bliss
Of the terrific two twirling in tandem
Why can't Paul
Walk hand in hand with Hippocrates on life's complex stage
And enlighten the innocent on holistic health?

When life's lot questions our clarity on critical things

And challenges our grasp of fundamental fits
Why favour the one and discard the other?
Why esteem the one and eject the other?

Are they not the caring Father's blessed keys
Given to all men and women
To face the challenges of life and living
And of the challenges of mystery and miracle?

When the loving God
Did not wish to strangle reason and fetter faith
Why do the so called wise men in this groaning world
Run around all day and all night
To privilege the one and push the other
Into the pit of their own making?

A truly wise and a blessed man discards neither
Receives them as the Maker's twin gifts
Conferred on all men and women
For a happy, healthy and a harmonious life

So let no one show contempt for scans, sutures and systematic care
He who plays with either
Ends up paying with his own life!

So dear Christian
Of your own accord
Do not snip at the delicate thread of life

Instead let the loving God lead you
To fulfil his will
To His glorious ripe-old-age full!

Sin and the Saviour

Like the tiger crouching patiently in the tall grass
Eyes glistening in the dark like liquid Emerald
Poised to leap on innocent and unsuspecting prey
Sin lurks at the door of everyday life!

Who can alert us?
But the one who neither slumbers
Nor knows what a shut-eye means

Who can guard us?
But the good shepherd of a hundred – plus sheep.
Carrying the weak in this loving arms
And keeping a watchful eye on the vulnerable

Who can save us?
But the sinless One and the Son of God

Who can help us?
But the One interceding for us Single-mindedly and ceaselessly

So, you and I
All men and women in this faithless fatalistic and fallen world
Let us run to the safety and shelter of God's Own son!
And the boundless grace of the merciful one!

The Dimensions of the Cross

Like the Challenger Deep
Swallowing Mount Everest in one big gulp
The cross subsumes, submerges and sinks
Umpteen challenges it encounters
Who can escape the gravity of this profound truth?

They who bear the cross
Will wear the corona
The doctors as well as the nurses
The sanitation workers as well as the security personnel
Indeed, all the corona warriors

Has the composer spewed lies?

Dear reader, India threw open
Five-star suites for covid care
And did not India
Deploy the supersonic sukhoi
To shower flowers from this mean and mighty machine?
On the heroic men and women
Working in the significant houses of God
Where the sick, the shivering and the sinking
Are cared for and cured
For relief and joy in the days to come

When covid ran amok among nations many
And raced across the globe from end to end
The conscientious and the reflective
Searched deep within themselves
To see if dross and dust had settled there

Who can dump the cross into the deepest sea
That it may lay unseen by the eye and the spirit of men?

Who can dump the cross into the deepest deep
That it may not even Bob or float?
Indeed, the cross bounces leaps
And brings to light, in the ripeness of time
The thoughts and deeds of men!

That they may send supplications to the saviour above

The Greeks saw folly up there
And the chosen race encountered a stumbling block
But who can disdain the dimensions of the cross
As merely six by three two-piece work of wood
Placed on the shoulders of the doubtful saviour?

Then, let the innocent bring to mind
The cross experienced by the two-hundred plus nations
And that nations big and small
Were immobilized as if by Anaconda's asphyxiating maw

Who has fixed the outer edge of the universe?
Neither Job nor I!
Who can imagine the vastness of space?
Neither Eliphaz nor you!
Neither Bildad nor Zophar!
Neither Elihu nor the wisemen.

Let the names of the doctors as well as the nurses
And the names of the sanitation workers
As well as the security personnel
Resonate in the twinkling sky
For the cross they bore of many
And let the name of God's own son
Reverberate across the starry heavens
For the cross he bore for your sin, my sin
And for the sins of all mankind

Silence is Gold

Silence is the chamber of the heart in which
The love of the creator is contemplated

Silence is the garden in which
The latent talents of many young people bloom

Silence is the oyster in which
The pearls of wisdom are formed

Silence is the womb in which
The child of invention and artistry is born

Silence is the island of tranquility in which
Mozart of Madras' melodious music is made

Silence is the fertile field in which
The seeds of wisdom are grown

But alas! My kingdom has been invaded
By a gang of boisterous brats!
My alcove has been hijacked
By a cacophony of Kilkenny cats!

Mighty God!
I plead with you! I beseech you! I implore you!

Rescue me from this irresistible army
For one silent hour
I would readily, most joyfully trade
All my glittering gold!!

Have Lots, Will Speak

In the hands of our loving impartial God are lots of wisdom
That spreads peace to every man and women that seeks
His blessed will among men
And bring this precious gift to every haunt and every home

My friend, who can deny it?

Heaven is light years away from politics on earth below
Where angels have time not for politics but only for praise

For too long, nay for ages have men
Coveted the seat of Ceasar
Only to fall between the stool of ambition
And the stool of termite envy

In the Lord's holy temple
No one is a rival to be overthrown
There is no team A or team B
Can't you see, dear child of God
Rivals there are none in the Lord's sanctuary

Did the creator call for campaigns that cleave Christ's body?

Dear friend, there is only God's plan of working in harmony
To be overseen by men full of maturity

There are no thrones to usurp
No seats to seize
Only sand near the sea of Galilee
To stand and hearken to the voice of wisdom
A small space at the foothills of the mountain
To savour the beatitudes daily
And a spot in the synagogue
To reverentially receive the salvation story

Everyone is of the same height
To the Lord who is in heaven enthroned
Everyone is of the same weight
To the Christ who is on the cross crucified

By a simple, single pick from the bunch
Now in hand and now lying a little scattered on the table
You revealed O Lord
Your unambiguous and clear will

The lots were nimble enough to pick our - iniquities - carrying scapegoat
Catch the escapist who sailed to Tarshish in the big boat
And choose the super sub for the mammon – serving turncoat

The roster was by the draw of lots made
Setting the teachers and the taught on the same circle
For an outpouring of singing and praise

The lots is a divine agency
No privilege it knows
No rank it recognizes
It only knows we are mere creatures

Order and peace you decreed O God
In the home and in the world
Fellowship and harmony in your place, you looked for O God
But alas! You found subterranean surges instead

In his left hand, he holds his body's peace
And with folded hands, the saviour with his father intercedes
That delicate veins, may not, in any place, bleed

With the spark of the spirit
Let us make a bonfire of the papers
Take a handful from the powdery heap
Sprinkle it on our cloth of remorse
Bow our heads in contrition
That we may joyfully don
The raiment of a renewed mind and the raiment of a renewed life

Your spirit makes clear to us O God that
You nailed nepotism to the cross
And purified the prejudice of the propagandist and the petty
The cronyism of the unconscionable Christian
You cleansed with your precious blood
To bless the Jew and the Gentile

The slave and the free

Men and women you did not forget
Any benediction you did not withhold
Such precious gifts you O Lord
Always wish men may share with all

Dreams for a Daughter Dear

Let not dear sister
Your precious tears wash away into the depths of Bay of Bengal
The dreams for your daughter dear

Let not loving sister
Boulders of badluck crush into powdered charcoal
The delicate dreams for your daughter dear

Dear sister, you toiled day in and day out
Selling soda in the blazing sun
And running a restaurant without even a decent break
Moving from place to place in Destiny's Central City
To weave in threads of gold
Dreams for your daughter dear

Alas! Your other half's misadventure in the city of pearls
Melted the mini mountain of fortune
Bringing misery in its wake
And dragging you down
To the arid land you left long long ago

Let not your misfortune shatter you dear sister
Let not your heart sink
Like a dinghy hit by a hurricane

And let not your hope crumble
Like millennium old walls

May the Lord up there
Shield you from the storms of life
And may the loving God who sees you
Restore your disintegrating dreams

May the Lord who made you and hears your prayers
On the day of your wonderful victory
That is, on the day of your daughter's memorable valedictory
Turn your burning tears that have flooded your face
Into pearls of everlasting praise!!

Breakfast Time Unshackled

The hurdles of life are knocked down
One after another
By resurrection's irresistible force
Giving me a time of grace for prayer in the morning
Instead of baking the bread of affliction
And of granting me a time of grace for praise in the evening
Instead of breaking the bread of affliction

The shackles of time are shattered into smithereens
By God the destroyer of obstacles big and obstacles small
What problem on earth can withstand
The Lord's decisive death-dealing blow to all things
Deemed undoable by the innocent many

There's no such lie
In the Lord's hope – giving book!

Resurrection gives a loud laugh
Crashing the gate impenetrable
Like the shouts that brought down the walls of Jericho!

The resurrection brings
A bagful of blessings by mercy mail
A hammer for me to pound and break the shackles of time
Until they are powder under my once-hurting feet

O how I cried and prayed and waited
With misty eyes like Hannah to witness a miracle

Indeed he baked the bread of sorghum every night
For sixty strength – sapping minutes
Content to eat the bread of affliction

Every night turned into a test and a trial
Relentlessly rolling on for years
Until his strength and his will almost snapped

At that trying moment
Walked the man whom the saviour sent
With the key that unlocked my feet and my future
Offering me
The time of my life for works exciting
Inviting me to immerse myself in
And enjoy every moment of my waking life

The Lord shares his dew with me
To turn the leaf of my life anew

The saviour puts the broken wheat and the broken sorghum
On the idli-cooking crucible
To serve me rupee-saving and time-slashing breakfast
Renewing my cells, skin and stagnating life
And before me spreads

A big blank sheet on a table
And hands me a pen full of ink
And vanishes into the cloud-laced sky

Resurrection brings a bagful of blessings by mercy mail
A hammer for me to pound and break the shackles of time
That I may throw them into Hell's fiery lake!!

What's in it for you, dear mate?

Ground Zero

I have no level to maintain
No catching up to do with the Joneses
I need no gauge!

Right before my very eyes
The King of kings at my feet in surreal simplicity lies
In the manger surrounded by curious eyes

Royal palaces you disdained O God
Cozy comforts you shunned
How deep are your ways O Father
That your son in our own form came
That we may behold and hold him
Like Simeon in our arms
And wonder and work on our imperfect ways

When foxes had their rest
And birds their nests
You a refugee's fate shared
And your oneness in suffering expressed
To lay bare the open-to-the-sky state of man

The Lord speaks the incarnate truth
To all those who care to ponder
The depths of values yonder!

The king of kings and the Lord of Lords
Hits the ground running
The wise men come searching
Carrying with them gold, frankincense and myrrh

The King of kings and the Lord of lords
Hits the ground running
Sending the snobbish and the showy
Spinning into the bottomless pit
To show all that glitters is for the innocent!
And all that glitters is not gold!

The Lord is incarnate
He levels every hill
And sets every valley with stepping stones of wisdom
So fashion the highway of humility, simplicity and wholeness
That the innocent may become pilgrims
And march to the temple of self-emptying love.

A Volatile Mix

Freedom is a gift of gold from God
That will lose its lustre
The moment man transgresses God's holy command

Alas! In the quick sands of the glamorous and the glitzy
Are the fetters of freedom concealed
Sucking the strayer
When he gallops on a tour of the tempting and the tantalizing

Into the freedom you gave him Lord he rushes and falls
Nine times out of ten
The head floundering, the legs flailing in a miserable stall

And on the rebound returns it to you O Lord
He rejects it not

Who can give a wide berth to them
But the spirit filled and the spirit guided

Why should a man possess this gift
Only to be swept away by the gale of temptation?

Why should he have this gift?
Only to end up as a gaffe?

Why should any man pay compound interest to the deceiver?

Let not the man with the green card of freedom
Wander in the land of the flesh and get enmeshed
Sin's sights are ever before him
Enticing the weak and the vulnerable
For a leisurely round of its smoky spaces and playboy pleasures

By the wayside let him park
By the power of the spirit, the street car named desire
That he may escape by more than a hair's breath
The scents, sounds and seductions
Of this enticing, ensnaring World

From the Israelites greatest king of the long list beyond
Have fallen prey
Bringing gnawing guilt in its train
Breaking him down into a million bits
And flooding his heart and eyes with heavy water grief

Make man a bondsman of your spirit O Lord
That he may harness liberty for life, not death
And that he may harness freedom for fullness, not for the Fall

Let him then not abandon the spirit's suit
Donning it for years stretching into decades
Until his last hour on this enticing, ensnaring world!

Passing into Nothingness

A thoughtful caring one
Picks up a pen to share his love
With children lying on misfortune's street
His many moments occupied
By thoughts of their up and heavy lift

He prayed and cared
And penned missives
That were not small at all

Back and forth they went
For seasons many

Then one unfine day
It all stops dead on the tracks of the moonless night!

A thick parcel of pages
Slip out one after another
Everyone finds one
I mean all the special three
Everyone has his leaf of gold!

The thoughtful caring one
Searches eagerly to check
If there is just one loving leaf for him

But finds a packet full of vacuum instead!

How quickly the double bond unbinds
How easily the loving bond is loosed
Did not the now grown-up child find
At least a torn piece of paper
Lying on the floor of the study room
To pen pressing matters?
To share happy times?

So, dear folks
All the caring and the sharing
In this strange wide world
Passes invariably into nothingness!

Peace of God

Peace of God is when
Miss Evening shows up in the morning
To stay through noon
Heaving and helping
Everyday

Peace of God is when
Cutting and chopping
Dicing and slicing
Filling and frying
Sieving and serving happens
To cook the food of life!

Peace of God is when
Juice is in the glass
Fruit is in the bowl
Food is on the plate
And when no meal is ever late!

Peace of God is when
The helping hand is,
Just a shout
Nay, just a call away!
To reach us in times of need

Let such peace abide
That we may draw water
From the wells of wonder
And from the wells of praise!

The Way of Wisdom

When there's a national fete or a popular festival
Birthday party or a lavish wedding
And when many a VIP may grace the occasion
To take their allotted place

Let me while the innocent men
Eye the centre spot and the photo op
Show myself as Christ's dear child
Carrying the Lord's words of wisdom in my heart
And seamlessly converting them into blessed deed.

Why should I shove my brothers and sisters
To snatch the spotlight?
For did not our Lord
Dip into the huge
vat of wisdom
And urge his audience to shun the spotlight?

So before the host of the wedding banquet
Can shunt me from the coveted seat
Let me hasten to the row's end
And plump for the seat zero

Here and beyond here lies Christ's ever-present cushion
Where a mighty fall from thoughtless self-promotion is insured
And where our Lord's promised blessing is assured

Let your loosed outer robe our self-pride unshackle
And blood from your nail-pierced hands
Wash away dross of our snobbish strut

For service you called us O Lord
Not servitude to worldly values
How it's done you O Lord a demo gave
Right before your disciple's eyes

So let your sublime heavenly wisdom
And our faithful life-changing witness
Carry on with renewed vigour
Until we are catapulted into the clouds of everlasting bliss!

The Rising Sun

You send your light on me everyday
That I may bask yet not be baked!

You touch me everyday
That I may face the sun yet not be fried!

You shine on me everyday
That I may glow yet not be grilled

You reach me soft
As not to roast
By passing walls
That stand so tall

Turning till I find a spot
Staying still I have my fill
Of the daily dose of vitamin D

You give me climes
That help me breathe
And grant me times
That hinder freeze

So, praise to you, O gracious God You truly are the Rising Sun

Under His Wings

I have travelled the long torturous road of two
These years have been a testing time

I count every hour, every minute every second
Why shouldn't I?
How many did you get?
Can you tell me exactly
How many they make?

Dear reader, this isn't fake psychology!

The storm of fate
Has blown away my mother and my mate

When I about my shelter brood
Just in time, a mother hen
Gathers me under her secure wings
With words of assurance of a home for me and my daughters dear
And as a double blessing, a kind and godly company

Though I am a mother of two lovely daughters
I am a baby hen for now, at least
I seek shelter under the rock of my salvation
He will be my fortress and my strength
For now and forever more

About the Author

BASA ENOCH ANAND ELEAZAR

Basa Enoch Anand Eleazar was born on 4th October 1967. He completed his Master's degree in English Literature from the Hyderabad Central University in 1991. He joined the United Theological College, Bangalore and finished the Bachelor of Divinity course in 1996.

From 1997 to 1998, he edited a Christian booklet,which was distributed to students in a few schools in Hyderabad.

He discontinued his work as editor as his condition of Ankylosing Spondylitis became more acute.

From 1998 to 2019, he preached in his church both in telugu and English with breaks as he aslo suffered later from Irritable bowel syndrome and hyponaetremia.

He stays at home and loves listening to the national and international news and songs based on classical ragas. His hobbies are chess and reading.

He has published a book in 2021 titled PEOPLE OF GOD SUFFERING,AND OTHER POEMS.

www.ingramcontent.com/pod-product-compliance
Lightning Source LLC
LaVergne TN
LVHW041641070526
838199LV00053B/3499